ELECTRIC GUITARS F(

Learn to Play Essential Rock Riffs

FREDERICK JOHNSON

Essential Guitar Chords Char
[u*se as reference*]

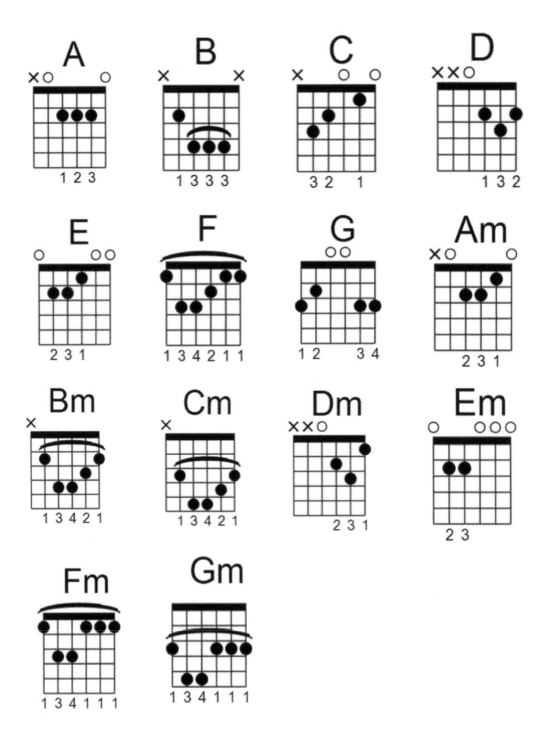

INTRODUCTION

Welcome to 'Essential Rock Riffs', the no-nonsense beginner's guide to playing rock music for those starting out. Very few guitar books and guides take you by the hand and provide you the thorough steps towards mastering the necessary techniques and basics of riffing. That's where I come in.

When I started playing guitar, it felt like everyone and their brother was better than me. I aspired to play like Cobain and Hendrix and wish I had a book like this one to help me understand what makes their playing so special, and how to replicate it. It took me years to forge my own style by taking the best of each of my favorite guitarists. Luckily, you don't have to wait years. Everything you need is in THIS guide.

What you will find in the following pages are the basics of reading tablature, how to play 'power chords', understanding riffing in every key and a whole bunch of awesome riffs inspired by the greatest of the greats. I urge you to come back to each riff once you've learned in and to repeat each one until you've mastered it. Practice, practice, practice!

So grab your guitar, tune up in standard E tuning, and let's begin.

TUNING UP

It's crucial to be in tune when playing. I've had many students over the years who think that because they tuned their guitar yesterday, they're ready to jam! Not true. Get into the good habit of tuning every time you play and your bandmates will thank you later (especially your bassist). A well tuned guitar does wonders for your overall sound. Every riff in this book is in standard tuning. This is also known as E standard.

Your lowest string is E and your highest string is E as well. It looks like this:

E standard tuning from low (left) to high (right).

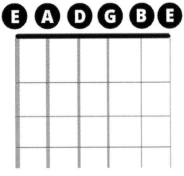

In order to get an accurate and precise tuning, I always recommend that you tune your guitar twice, going over each string two times to ensure that you're all set for your lessons and jam sessions. These days, you don't need a traditional tuner and it's far easier to download a free tuning app from your smartphone/tablet's respective app store.

ESSENTIAL ELECTRIC GUITAR CHORDS

Before we get going with the riffs themselves, in this initial chapter, we're going to be talking about chords on the electric guitar in general. There are many misconceptions about guitar chords that not many beginner guitarists are taught when they first start out. The primary and biggest of these, is that you can strum and play the same chords on an acoustic that you can on an electric. This is not entirely true because the technique is different! Allow me to explain.

While you can obviously play the same chord shapes on both types on guitar, that doesn't mean the way that you play them is the same. The way that electric and acoustic guitars are designed is completely different. The acoustic is, by nature, a much more 'strum' friendly instrument in that you can be more flexible with how powerfully you strum it – since it is hollow bodied. I've seen a lot of beginners (who started on an acoustic and then moved onto an electric) strum chords the same way on both! This is wrong. Electric guitars are far more delicate and when you strum them as powerfully as you would an acoustic guitar, you get a distorted and muffled sound that doesn't sound pleasing to the ear.

What I am getting at is the fact that electric guitars are to be strummed more lightly. As a result, open chords (standard chords) don't sound as good on them. The solution, in my opinion, and that I've found, is changing how you play chords. That is, by changing the fingering of the chord to match the tone and delicacy of an electric guitar. That is where the unusual and unique chord shapes that you'll learn in this book come in handy – they're absolutely electric guitar friendly by design.

The first step to learning electric guitar chords is to understand that you down 'powerhouse' your strumming in an aggressive way, like you would on an acoustic. Of course there are many exceptions – particularly for certain kinds of metal, djent, punk rock and so on.

Now for the upcoming essential rock riffs, you need to understand the MAIN type of chord that rockers use. Power chords.

POWER CHORDS & TABLATURE

So now that your guitar is in tune and we have dealt with all the basics of guitar housekeeping, maintenance and the different parts, it's time to get to actually playing the guitar. In this chapter, we will be exploring tablature and all that you need to know about tabs – reading them, writing them out and what they mean. In the simplest terms, tablature (or 'tabs' for short) are what guitarists use to read music. You'll need this to play the riffs in the subsequent pages.

It is a simplified version of sheet music and is relatively straight forward to comprehend once you understand the basic principles behind it.

Take a look at this diagram:

(diagram a)

```
E
B   T
G
D   A
A
E   B
```

This is a 'tab', and it is what we use in guitar music to indicate where we should place our fingers and what note to play. There are usually numbers on the lines to indicate this.

The line at the very top (above the *T* of *TAB* in the diagram above) is the high E – the thinnest and highest pitch string of the guitar and the E at the bottom is the low E and so, tabs are read from the bottom up and not the top up. The number on the string indicates the fret we play on the fretboard.

Therefore, a '0' indicates that we are to play an open string without pressing on the fretboard. The diagram above doesn't have any notes on it and therefore is just a tablature stave. In cases where notes are played, the fret number (that is, the fret you play) will be written on the appropriate string.

Take a look at the diagram below which demonstrates a tab with actual notes on it.

(diagram b)

In this diagram, you should see three separate notes. The (1) on the low string, the (3) on the next string, and yet another (3) which is indicated on the string that follows it. The numbers indicate which fret you play (if you are still unsure what a fret is, please do   refer to the annotated diagram on page 4). In the case of this melody, each note is separated and not grouped which means we play them individually as opposed to playing them together which would make a chord (but more on this later). In order to play this tune, place your index finger on the first fret of the low string (E string). Next, use your ring finger (fourth finger) on the third fret of the A string and finish by playing the third fret of the D string with your pinky finger.

The notes in the melody we just looked at can also be grouped. This forms a power chord. Essentially, by playing all three notes at once, we form a small version of a chord which is called a power chord.

Take a look at the following version of the same notes we just played.

(diagram c)

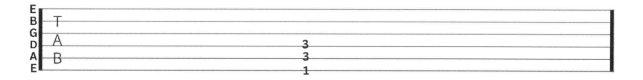

This chord is called an F power chord which means it is a short version of the long F chord. This is our first 'chord' but written in the form of a tab. Long versions of chords are called 'open' chords but for rock, power chords are usually preferable, especially when combining them with riffs. Now you should know the difference between individual notes for riffs (as we saw in *diagram b*) and power chords when you group them like in *diagram c* on the previous page. In order to play the chord in this tab, follow the instructions below.

Step 1: Place your index finger on the first fret of the low E string.

Step 2: Place your ring finger on the third fret of the A string.

Step 3: Place your pinky on the third fret of the D string.

Step 4: Strum (with your right hand) the top three strings.

This is a power chord and the shape that your fingers are in can be transposed anywhere on the fretboard to create different power chords, which are essential for riffs, which we will come to later.

Moving the same shape up from the first fret to the third fret creates a G power chord. It looks like this:

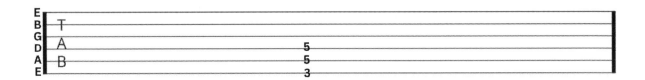

One more example... this time on the A string. Here is a C power chord with the root note on the A string. Place your index finger on the third fret of the A string, your ring finger on the fifth fret of the D string and your pinky on the fifth fret of the D string. It's exactly the same as the G power chord but every finger moves down one string. This shape can be used anywhere on the fretboard with roots on the E or A strings, as long as you start with your index finger on the root note of origin (D power chord starts on the fifth fret of the A string, E power chord on the seventh of the A and so on).

Now that you understand basic tablature and power chord shapes, it's ALMOST time for the riffs. First for picking technique!

PICKING AND STRUMMING

It's all well and good to know what notes to play, but for many guitarists starting out, knowing HOW to play them can be tricky. I'm assuming you have a pick in your hand while you're reading this so let's get to the techniques for clean picking on electric guitar. You don't want to pick or strum too hard. Strumming is for chords, picking is for individual notes.

Picking and strumming patterns are an essential part of playing the guitar and make notes and chords sound either amazing or downright shoddy. When starting out on guitar, most players pick downwards on every stroke. This works for some riffs but upstrokes are just as important. When writing out picking patterns, guitarists use D (down pick) and U (up pick) to signify what sort of picking is used. Hold your pick between your thumb and index finger with the pointed end facing downwards towards the string. For many guitar riffs in this book, picking in a downwards (D) motion for every note will be just fine. But alternate patterns are also essential sometimes.

Try picking the open low E string in THIS alternate picking pattern:

D   U   D   U   D   U

(Down, up, down, up, down, up, down, up)

Use control in your picking and practice these patterns so you don't hit strings accidentally. Some mistakes are expected when you start but try and focus on accuracy and cleanly striking the note (NOT TOO HARD) without strumming notes that aren't part of a riff.

Now, let's try combining multiple notes with a picking pattern. For this next exercise, you will play the following three note riff using two picking patters. Let's start with all down strokes. So the pattern is

D   D   D

Give it a go:

Start with your index finger on the fretting hand on the fourth fret of the A string (second string down). With your picking hand, play it on a down stroke. Next on the fretting hand, play the sixth fret of the D string with your ring finger.

With your picking hand, play it on a downstroke and finally, play the sixth fret of the G string (next string down) with your pinky and pick it downwards as well.

Now it's time for something slightly harder. Play the same riff with this picking pattern:

D   D   U

Follow the same steps from the previous page with only ONE MAJOR DIFFERENCE! On the last note instead of picking the final note in a downwards motion, you want to strum an upwards motion with your pick. Down, down, UP. Sometimes, down and up are symbolised with arrows in tablature: ↑ for up-pick, and ↓ for down.

Give it a go:

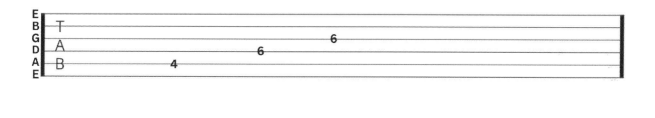

Fancy a challenge?

I've noticed that you're a natural! A real rockstar in the making. So how about we try some more challenging picking patterns. Using the riff we just practiced, or any configuration of the three individual notes that make up power chords across the fretboard, try the picking patterns on the following page.

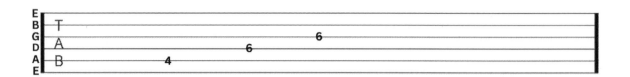

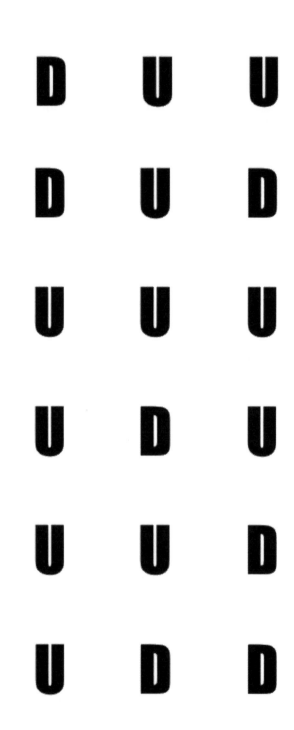

LEVEL ONE : PRACTICE RIFFS

If you want to cut to the chase and start rocking out to the big ones, skip this chapter and dive right into the main rock riffs of the book. However, for those who need a bit more practice and want to start easy, this section is for you. We're going to start with some practice riffs. Very basic, easy riffs to get you started. No frills, just straight forward fingering patterns.

Practice Riff #1

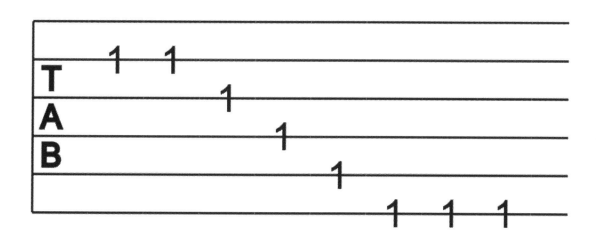

This riff is designed to get you accustomed to switching strings in a riff. Instead of starting on the lower strings, this one begins on the B string and works it's way up to the low E string. Everything is on the first fret so it's not too complicated! Take your time.

Top rocker's tip: you can use your index finger for the whole riff!

Practice Riff #2

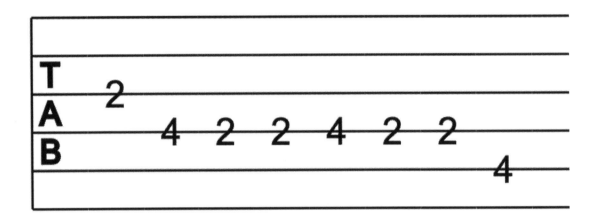

This one is in F# and uses less strings. Start slow, but the aim of this riff is to eventually build up speed and good picking technique.

We start on the second fret of the G string (fourth string down) with our index finger. You want to <u>down</u> pick this note.

That means with your OTHER hand (picking hand), holding your pick between your thumb and index finger, strum the string in a downwards motion.

Then, with your ring finger, play the fourth fret of the D string (third string down), the second fret of the same string with your index finger (twice), then back to the fourth fret and play the second fret twice once more before finishing the riff on the fourth fret of the A string (second string down and second lowest in pitch) with your ring finger.

Practice Riff #3

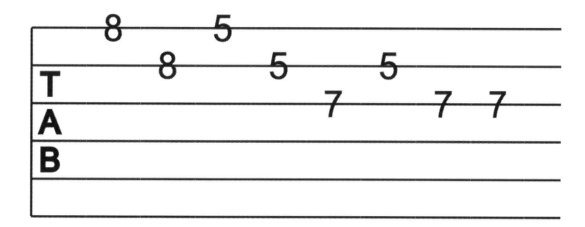

The focus of this riff is the higher strings.

Practice Riff #4

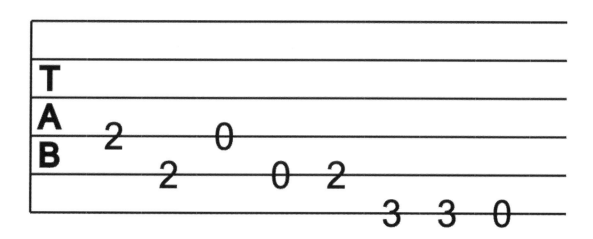

And now the lower strings. This one is more on the rock end of things. Remember to go back and familiarize yourself with picking patterns. It might help to start on a down stroke but only YOU can determine which patterns work for you.

Practice Riff #5

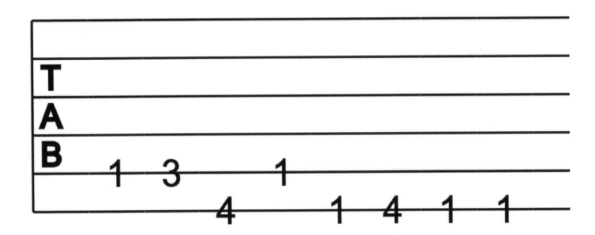

Practice Riff #6

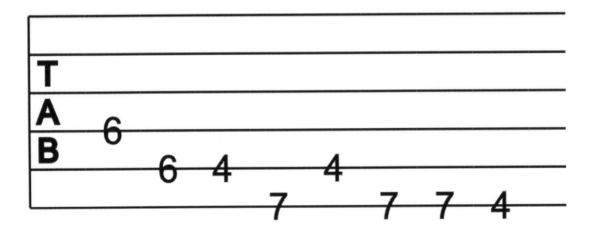

Need some help with this one? It might aid you to know that when you have a riff that starts on a higher fret before going down to lower frets (in this case, starting on the sixth fret and going down to the fourth), start the riff with your ring finger so your index finger is naturally placed to play the lower frets closer to the headstock.

Practice Riff #7

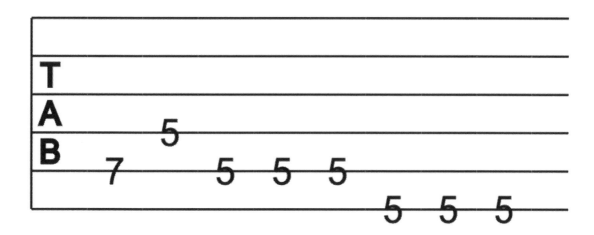

Practice Riff #8

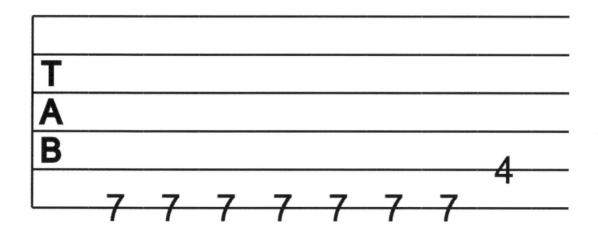

So now that we've completed the introductory course, you're about to learn to play some of the coolest rock riffs. Congratulations! Remember to take your time and to refer to the introduction of this book when in doubt. Don't forget that practice makes perfect! It's okay to be frustrated sometimes and to feel like you aren't making progress, but believe me when I say that you absolutely are.

Embarking on the journey of learning electric guitar is an exhilarating adventure filled with endless possibilities. Here are some final tips before we get to the riffs:

- *As a beginner, remember to embrace patience and persistence. Start by mastering the fundamentals such as proper hand positioning, fretting technique, and understanding basic chords.*

- *Consistency in practice is key; even short, regular sessions can yield significant progress over time.*

- *Don't hesitate to explore various musical styles within the genres you're interested in (in this case, ROCK). This will enable you to broaden your horizons and discover your unique sound.*

- *Set achievable goals and celebrate your victories along the way, no matter how small they may seem. Embrace the inevitable challenges as opportunities for growth and learning.*

- *Surround yourself with fellow musicians as your jam sessions will be the most productive place to learn band dynamics and to grow as a guitarist and overall musician.*

- *Let your passion for music fuel your dedication, and never lose sight of the joy and fulfilment that comes from expressing yourself through the power of the electric guitar. Remember, every great guitarist was once a beginner with a dream…*

LEVEL TWO: ESSENTIAL ROCK TECHNIQUES

PALM MUTING

Just a few final techniques that you need to know. Palm muting is a technique signified by *PM* in tablature. Commonly used in rock, metal, and other genres to create a percussive, muted sound, it involves using the fleshy part of your picking hand (palm) to lightly touch the strings near the bridge while you pick or strum the strings with your other hand. Rest the fleshy part of your palm lightly on the strings just in front of the bridge. Your hand should be relaxed but firm enough to make contact with the strings. For picking technique, use your other hand to pick or strum the strings as you normally would. However, keep in mind that the palm-muted strings should produce a short, muted sound rather than ringing out clearly. Experiment with the amount of pressure you apply with your palm.

PULL-OFFS AND HAMMER-ONS

Pull-offs and hammer-ons are two common techniques used in guitar playing to articulate notes without picking each individual note separately. They're often used in conjunction with picking to create fluid, legato lines and add expressiveness to your playing. Let's break down each technique:

Hammer-ons:

A hammer-on is a technique where you play a note by "hammering" your finger down onto a fretboard without picking the string.

To perform a hammer-on:

STEP ONE: Start by fretting a note on a string with your fretting hand. Let's use the third fret of the A string with our index finger.

STEP TWO: Next, with your ring finger of the same hand, firmly press down the fifth fret of the same string without plucking the string with your other hand.

The force of your finger pressing down on the fret will cause the string to vibrate and produce the note. Hammer-ons are typically denoted in guitar tablature with the letter 'h' between the notes (e.g 5h7 on the same string would mean hammering on from the 5th fret to the 7th fret).

```
T
A
B              5      h      7
```

Now for pull-offs!

A pull-off is the opposite of a hammer-on. It's a technique where you play a note by "pulling" your finger off a fret while maintaining contact with the string to produce another note.

To perform a pull-off:

STEP ONE: Start by placing your index finger of your fretting hand on the second fret of the A string and your ring finger on the fourth fret in front of it on the same string. Pluck the string.

STEP TWO: Next, without picking the string again with your picking hand, quickly and forcefully pull your ring finger off the fret to reveal the note fretted behind it – the second fret of the A string.

The motion should be quick and deliberate to ensure the pulled-off note rings out clearly.

Pull-offs are typically denoted in guitar tablature with the letter 'p' between the notes.

Both techniques require practice to develop speed, accuracy, and control. Start slowly and focus on getting clean, clear notes. Gradually increase your speed as you become more comfortable with the technique. Experiment with different finger combinations and sequences to develop dexterity. Now for the moment you've been waiting for… the ROCK RIFFS!

ESSENTIAL ROCK RIFFS

Dragonfly Dance

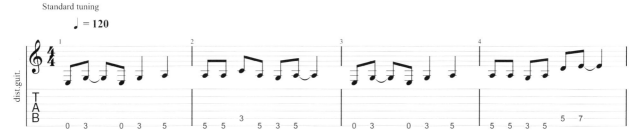

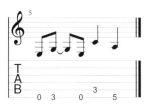

Rockin´ Rain

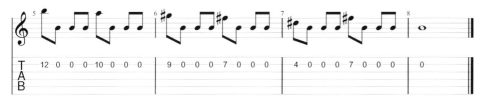

Funky Spy Groove

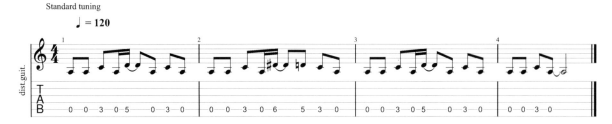

Dino Boogie

Mermaid Melody

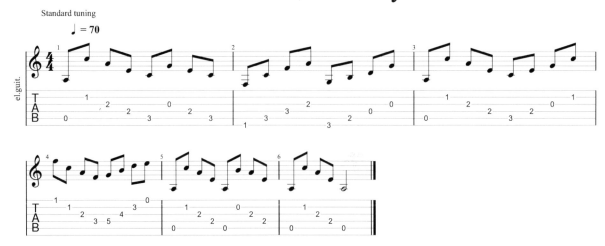

Robot Rock 'n Roll

Knight's Quest Quake

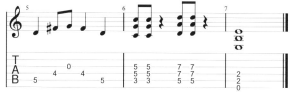

Pirate Party Anthem

Magical Mystery Train Ride

White Knight

Alien Adventure Anthem

Jungle Jamboree

Sky High Swing

Steamy Serenade

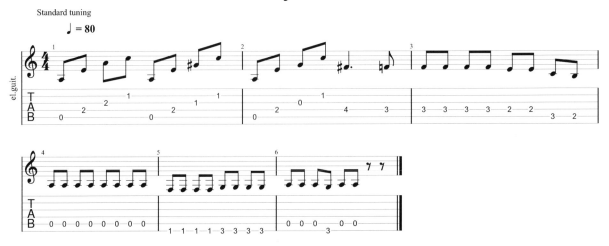

Rock All Day

Clock Rock

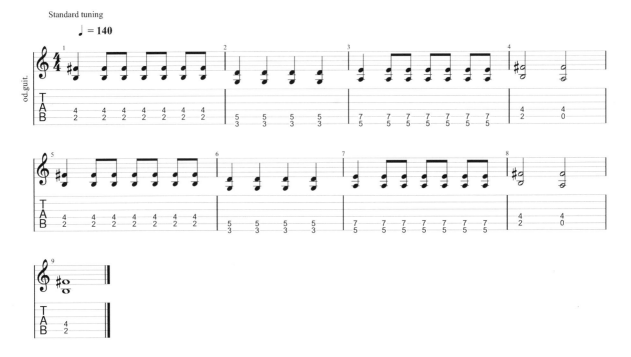

Back To Home

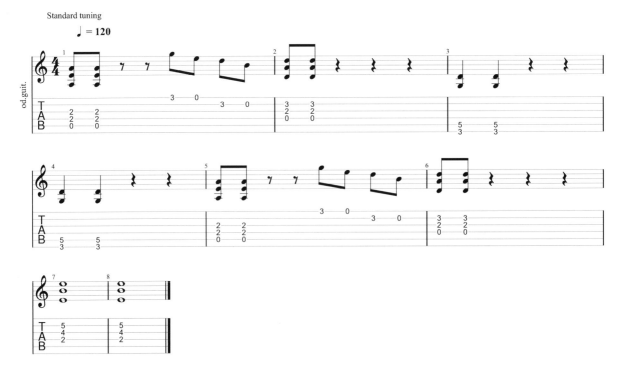

Wild West Whirlwind

Under The Sea

Monster Mash Meltdown

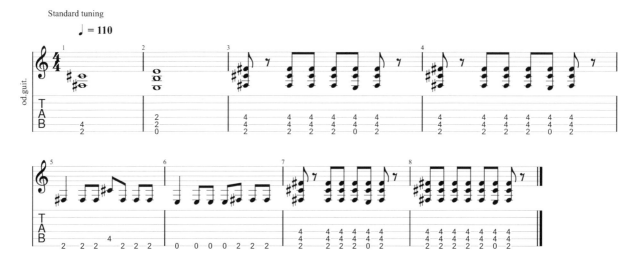

Far Away

Space Explorer Strut

Magical Mouse Melody

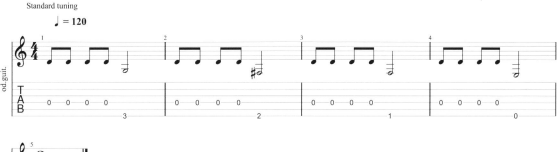

Pirate Parrot Party

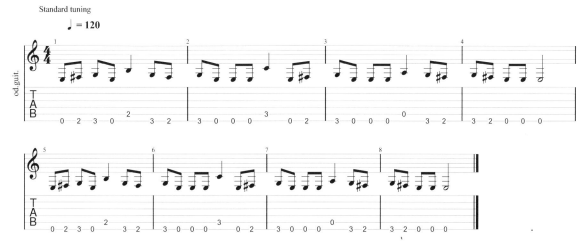

Time Traveling T-Rex Tango

Adventurous Antics Anthem

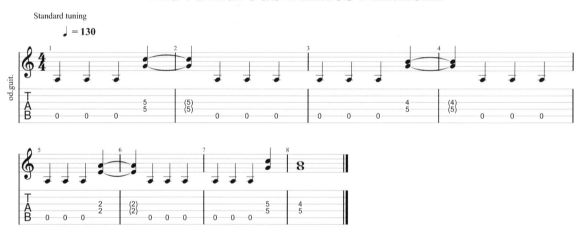

Whimsical Whale Waltz

Adventurous Aardvark Anthem

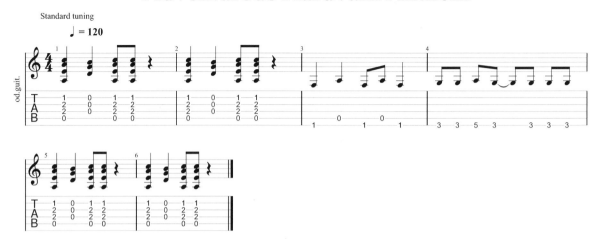

Superhero Shuffle Showdown

Rockin' Raccoon Rhythms

Congratulations! You've completed the first section of essential riffs. Now we're going to take it up a notch and learn some harder ones that include some of the more advanced techniques that we learned in the course section at the start of the book!

Four Step Blues Rock

Whole Lotta Josie

Bulls On Patrol

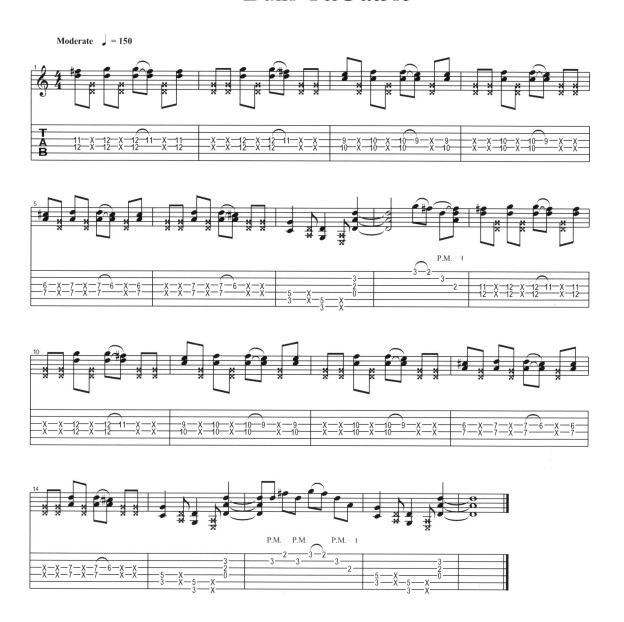

Flamingo Jammin'

Gary's Got A New Strat

Serpentine

Mamma Said

Take Her Out Tonight

Rum n' Coke

A&M Publishing

Frederick Johnson

Made in United States
Orlando, FL
17 June 2025

62179819R00028